HIGHER EDUCATION FOR WOMEN IN GREAT BRITAIN

This edition published by Lector House in 2024

ISBN: 978-93-6138-239-0
Edition copyright © 2024 by Lector House LLP
All rights reserved under the International Copyright Conventions.

Lector House LLP
Registered Office: H. No. 96, Block C, Tomar Colony,
Burari, Delhi – 110084, India
info@lectorhouse.com
www.lectorhouse.com

HIGHER EDUCATION FOR WOMEN IN GREAT BRITAIN

PHOEBE SHEAVYN

2024

LECTOR HOUSE

LECTOR HOUSE LLP

HIGHER EDUCATION FOR WOMEN IN GREAT BRITAIN

BY

PHŒBE SHEAVYN, D. LIT. (LOND.).

Senior Tutor for Women Students,
(University of Manchester).

Contents

APPENDIX.

HIGHER EDUCATION FOR WOMEN IN GREAT BRITAIN

By PHOEBE SHEAVYN, D.Lit. (Lond.),

*Senior Tutor for Women Students,
University of Manchester.*

Introduction.

The movement for the education of girls is of recent growth, dating back less than a century, to the decade 1840-50. Before that time there was no public provision for them, educational endowments being used for boys only. The earliest tangible sign of the progress of the movement was the foundation in London of Queen's College, Bedford College and the North London Collegiate School for Girls, and in the provinces of the Cheltenham Ladies' College. This inaugurated the era of public secondary education for girls, who now have their large, well-equipped schools in every town.

At first the education given was necessarily very simple; but as the schoolgirls of the new age grew up, the need for a more extended training became apparent. It was met partly by an extension of the teaching given in certain of the schools; partly by the establishment of a system of lectures for older girls, notably at Queen's College, London, and in Glasgow, Liverpool and Manchester. Before long it became clear that some more systematic higher education must be provided, and efforts were made to enlist the sympathies of the Universities. University professors undertook to repeat their lectures for the benefit of girls; but the number of girls was for some time too few to finance these schemes, and it was apparent that either their numbers must be increased by the provision of residence, or expenses must be reduced by obtaining the admission of girls to the classes held for men. Both measures were attempted. A residential College for girls was established at Hitchin (1869), afterwards removed to Girton, near Cambridge (1873); Newnham Hall (later "College") was founded in Cambridge in 1871; and in Oxford, Lady Margaret Hall (1878) and Somerville Hall (later "College") (1879). Before long residence in or near London was provided by Bedford College, Westfield College, and the Royal Holloway College at Englefield Green in Surrey.

Meanwhile, a great impetus had been given in 1878 to the higher education of women throughout England by the opening to them of the examinations and degrees of the University of London. This University was at that time purely an examining body, and teaching had to be provided locally; but the possibility of obtaining the hall-mark of a University degree greatly increased the number of girls seeking instruction in the provincial towns, and many institutions gradually opened their doors, among the first being Owens College, afterwards the University of Manchester. At Glasgow, Queen Margaret College, availing itself largely of the services of University lecturers, was founded in 1883.

Further advance was marked by the statutory permission given in 1892 to the Scottish Universities, granting them power to admit women to graduation and to provide for their instruction. And in 1893 the Royal Charter for the new University of Wales definitely enacted that women should be eligible for all privileges accorded to men. Every University incorporated since that date has adopted a similar enactment. The last two strongholds of masculine privilege, Oxford and Cambridge, held out for many years. Quite recently, in 1920, Oxford has capitulated with a whole-hearted grace, which has won for this ancient University the gratitude of all women. Cambridge alone now still refuses to women the privilege of membership and graduation, but it cannot be long before there also admission will be granted. One may safely prophesy that the completion of the century (1940) will see the admission of women to full University rights.[1]

---

[1] Except a few privileges likely for some time to be reserved for men at Oxford and Cambridge, and certain which cannot legally be bestowed (*e.g.*, scholarships with special trust deeds limiting them to men).

The General Education System.

Elementary education is entirely free in public schools, supported jointly by the State and the Municipal and County Councils. Many of the good Secondary Schools, moreover, have preparatory departments, in which fees are charged; and there is a large number of private Kindergarten and other Preparatory Schools, charging small fees and offering a mediocre education. Middle-class parents prefer to send their children to these rather than to the public Elementary Schools, fearing possible contamination to morals and manners in the latter.

Secondary education in England and Wales is carried on in several classes of institution.

1. "High Schools," under the management of specially established educational corporations, pioneers in secondary education.

2. Endowed Schools—few in number for girls.

3. Municipal or County Schools—some for girls only, others for girls and boys. These have usually been started on a lower educational level; but they are rapidly improving, and many of them now give an education quite equal to that given by the good High Schools which led the way.

4. Private Schools; of which some are expensive, and excellently equipped and staffed; others expensive and poorly provided, relying mainly on their social prestige; others inexpensive and poor.

Many parents of the more wealthy or aristocratic families still entrust the education of their girls to private governesses, from whom they require chiefly a knowledge of languages and the usages of polite society, supplemented, perhaps, by music and painting. The movement for the more complete education of women has not as yet gained much strength among those sections of society in which a girl is not expected to earn her own living.

Teachers of the public schools are for the most part prepared professionally, after completing their Secondary School course, at special Training Colleges, supported by State and Municipal grants—in some cases supplemented by fees from the student. This professional course for teachers in Elementary Schools covers two years. In a few of the Universities also, arrangements are made for a two-year course; in others, however, only teachers for Secondary Schools are now prepared. These study first for their degree (Bachelor) during three years, following this up by a fourth year devoted to professional training. During the whole course the University fees are paid by the State through the Board of Education, and a substantial grant is made to the student for maintenance. Many women who could not otherwise meet the expense of a University career are thus enabled, at the cost of undertaking to teach for a certain number of years, to pass through the University practically without expense.

In some Universities, and particularly in those which still offer a two-year training course for teachers in Elementary Schools, the "training students" form a class somewhat apart from the others, regarded as to some extent socially, and perhaps also intellectually, inferior. In others no distinction whatever exists, except that the "training" student has to satisfy the fairly stringent regulations of the Board of Education, in regard to making satisfactory progress year by year.

Teachers in the preparatory departments of Secondary Schools have usually received a thorough professional training; but those in the small private Kindergartens have commonly very meagre qualifications.

In the better schools the education of girls is good, and though there is cause for complaint as to "overpressure," attention is given to the physical condition of the pupils; of late, it is becoming customary to have girls medically examined at school from time to time. Science and Mathematics are often not as well taught as in boys' and mixed schools; but the teaching has rapidly improved during the last decade, and a good deal of practical work is always included. In languages, much headway has been made and new methods are earnestly followed; but the general level of linguistic study is still below that in most continental countries. The general level of Secondary education is good; but the schools suffer from a multiplicity of external examinations, for which public opinion compels them to prepare pupils.

The more advanced pupils are prepared for the Entrance Examinations (usually called Matriculation) of the different Universities, and they afterwards compete for one of the many scholarships offered by the local educational authorities or by the Universities. Competition for these is very keen. Recently an examination of higher standard—for the "Higher Certificate"—has been instituted by the Board of Education, preparation for which is regarded as carrying on the school education to a level comparable with that of the first year at the University. It is still, however, in an experimental stage, and the amount of recognition to be awarded by the more conservative Universities is as yet uncertain.

The Board of Education is the Government Department, which concerns itself with the education of both boys and girls in all stages. It maintains an army of Inspectors, men and women, for schools of all types; it conducts examinations for Secondary Schools; and it makes arrangements, through Training Colleges founded by various bodies, for the professional training of teachers for both Elementary and Secondary Schools. It works for the most part through locally appointed Education Committees, paying grants to them for all Schools and Training Colleges under their control. It lays down a scale (or rather scales) of salaries to be paid to teachers in various types of Public School. The Board also undertakes, when requested, to inspect and certify as "efficient" schools privately conducted, but it does not exercise any supervision over the larger number of such schools. Recent regulations, raising the salaries of teachers in "State-aided" Schools, and providing good pensions, are likely to crush out of existence many of the less efficient of the private schools; some educationalists fear that even the more efficient may now find it difficult to secure good teachers; and they hold that in that case, valuable freedom of initiative in education may be lost to the nation.

The University Training Departments in the larger Universities regard it as part of their natural function to initiate new and experimental methods in education; and some of them have special schools established for the purpose. Excellent pioneer work of the kind is described in the records of the

Fielden School, under the University of Manchester. This University has established a Faculty of Education, in which one of the Professors devotes his whole time to the superintendence of the work of students for the research degree of Master of Education.

The Universities.

The Government and the Universities.—Universities in Great Britain enjoy a very considerable amount of freedom; in fact, the curriculum may be said to be entirely in the hands of the Academic Governing Body (called in most modern Universities, The Senate, but passing under various titles in the older Universities). Only such institutions as are incorporated by a University Charter from Government may grant degrees, but enactments in matters academic are made by the University itself, under the constitution as laid down in each Charter. The Government, through the Board of Education, makes yearly grants to Universities and Colleges; but it has hitherto refrained from laying down any stringent conditions as to the precise use made of them. The amount of the Government grant is however very small as compared with what is given in other countries, and higher education has to depend very largely upon endowment by private benefactors, with some support from municipal grants. The present critical state of national and private finance, together with the largely increased demand for higher education, has brought about in all Universities something like a serious financial crisis—for which at the present moment no adequate remedy appears.

Universities and Colleges.—There are no degree-giving Colleges in the United Kingdom; all degree-giving institutions are called Universities. Colleges are institutions too much specialised or too incomplete to be incorporated as Universities in themselves; they may form parts of a University, or may be independent. There are no degree-giving institutions for women only, as in the United States.

List of Universities and Colleges Open to Women.

Universities.—Birmingham, Bristol, Cambridge (partially open), Durham, Leeds, Liverpool, London, Manchester, Oxford, Sheffield, Wales; in Scotland—Aberdeen, St. Andrews, Edinburgh, Glasgow; in Ireland—Belfast, Dublin, the National University.

Colleges.—

(1) Forming part of a University.

In the University of St. Andrews:—University College, Dundee.

In the University of Durham:—University College; College of Medicine, Armstrong College—both at Newcastle-upon-Tyne.

In the University of London:—Bedford College, University College, King's College for Women, East London College, Royal Holloway College, Westfield College, London Day Training College, London School of Medicine for Women, School of Economics, School of Oriental Studies, etc., etc.

In the University of Manchester:—Municipal College of Technology.

In the University of Oxford:—Lady Margaret Hall, Somerville College, St. Hugh's College, St. Hilda's Hall, Society of Home Students.

In the University of Wales:—University College of Wales, Aberystwyth; University College of North Wales, Bangor; University College of South Wales, Cardiff; University College of Swansea.

In the University of Glasgow:—Queen Margaret College.

In the National University of Ireland:—University College, Cork; University College, Dublin; University College, Galway.

(2) Independent Colleges.

Girton College, Newnham College—preparing for the degree examinations of Cambridge University.

The Imperial College of Science and Technology (London)—preparing for its own Diplomas.

Exeter, Nottingham, Reading, Southampton Colleges—preparing for the degrees of the (External) University of London.

Where there are various Colleges within the University, it is customary to make application for admission to the University through the College selected.

Queen Margaret College is the name given to the women's side of the University of Glasgow; all applications from women for entrance to the University must be made through the College.

In Cambridge, all women students must be members of either Girton or Newnham College, and can only receive permission to attend University lectures or examinations through the College.

In Oxford, the body of Home Students ranks as a College, and has a Principal.

The following Universities are ancient foundations:—Cambridge, Oxford, Durham, Aberdeen, St. Andrews, Edinburgh, Glasgow, Belfast (Queen's College), and Dublin (Trinity College). The other Universities are grouped together as "Modern." The Scottish Universities, however, being chiefly non-residential, and situated in large cities, have many features in common with the modern group.

Teaching System.—At Oxford and Cambridge the system is a combination of University, Inter-Collegiate and College lectures, classes and seminars, with individual teaching. Each undergraduate student is under the personal guidance of a tutor or director of studies, who plans out her course of work for term and vacations, supervises her studies, advises her as to lectures, teaches her, either alone or with others, and arranges, if necessary, for additional tuition. Great importance is attached to written work (consisting in Oxford mainly of essays, in Cambridge in answers to question papers), and to a close personal relation between teacher and pupil. This system has obvious advantages to the student, as the tutor has scope for developing individual capacity, but it makes considerable demands upon the tutor's time. Science students are admitted to the University laboratories, both in

Cambridge and in Oxford, and in the former University, Natural Science is one of the subjects most popular and important. Advanced students obtain advice and supervision in their work from Professors and other specialists.

In other Universities, instruction is carried on mainly by means of lectures; the amount of written work is smaller, and there is practically no "coaching," either of individuals or of small groups—except where the number studying a given subject is extremely small. There is a trend of opinion in favour of the appointment of Tutors to give general guidance to those wishing for it, but the expense at present bars any innovation on a large scale in this direction. Some of the residential Halls provide tutors for their students. In all scientific subjects a considerable amount of practical work in the laboratories is required of the student, with more or less individual guidance from the Demonstrators in charge of the laboratories.

It is the vice of most of the modern Universities to require attendance at too large a number of lectures, leaving too little time for study and thought. And though the evil is readily recognised, and efforts are made from time to time to reduce the amount of attendance required, the zeal and autocratic power of the Professor in charge of any given subject has usually succeeded in defeating them.

In English Universities it is customary to call courses for a first degree either Honours or Pass Courses. The Honours Course is specialised—only one subject (say, a language or a science) with a minimum amount of one or two related subjects. A Pass Course is more general. Both types of Course cover, as a rule, a period of three years before the Final Degree Examination; which may, or may not, be preceded by subsidiary examinations in the earlier years. It is the rule in most of the Women's Colleges in Cambridge and Oxford that Honours Examinations only may be prepared for; in other Universities and Colleges, the women, like the men, can choose between Honours and Pass. There has been of late years a growing tendency to choose the more specialised course; it has more prestige, and the Headmistresses of Girls' Secondary Schools have preferred specialists as teachers. But there are slight indications that this preference is becoming less marked; and there may possibly before long be seen a revival of the demand for a more general education—which is manifestly suited to certain types of mind.

Degrees.—The degrees conferred by the Universities are those of Bachelor, Master, and Doctor. Not all of these degrees, are, however, conferred in every Faculty. The Course for a Bachelor's degree usually covers three years[2]; the Master's degree is sometimes (as in Oxford and Cambridge) conferred for a payment without further examination; sometimes, as in most of the modern Universities, it requires a further examination; in Scottish Universities it is the first degree, obtained after three years' study. Hence this degree connotes a surprising variety of attainment. The Doctor's degree is in all Universities awarded only upon the production of original work which can be regarded as a serious contribution to knowledge.

Recently every University has created a Ph.D. degree, open to graduates of any approved institution, British or foreign. It is given for advanced work only, the results of which must be embodied in a dissertation; and study must have been prosecuted during the greater part of two (or three) years in the University conferring the degree. It may be conferred in any Faculty. Many of the other higher degrees, M.A., M.Sc., B.Litt., etc., etc., are also open to graduates from other approved institutions.

The Imperial College of Science and Technology, London, holds a special position among independent Colleges, granting a diploma of its own which is regarded as equal in standard to a University degree.

Subjects Studied.—The greater number of women students enter the Faculty of Arts, but large numbers also enter for Science and for Medicine; a few for Commerce, Technology, Law, etc. The study of Medicine can now be carried on under the same conditions as for men in practically all the modern Universities. In some, however, situated in comparatively small towns, the clinical facilities are inadequate, and it is customary to continue clinical study in one of the larger Medical Schools, London, Edinburgh, Glasgow, Liverpool, or Manchester. Edinburgh, with a long-established prestige in medicine, attracts large numbers of students. Tradition inherited from early days of controversy has long limited the opportunities of women in Edinburgh, but a more liberal policy now admits them to substantial privileges.

In London, the position of medical study is peculiar. It is mainly in the hands of ancient Medical Schools, each with its own large Hospital—Bartholomew's, St. George's, Guy's, St. Thomas's, Westminster, etc.—out of

---

[2] In Cambridge the examination for the first degree is called the "Tripos"; in Oxford it is called "Schools."

which, in fact, the Teaching School has developed. These great Medical Schools followed the policy of the University of Edinburgh, opposing to the admission of women such relentless hostility that eventually the women had to create and finance a separate school. Thus came into being the London School of Medicine for Women, which succeeded in making a working arrangement for clinical instruction at the Royal Free Hospital. Though women are now admitted to the Medical Schools of University and King's Colleges, and the Charing Cross Hospital, most of the great Hospital Medical Schools are still closed to them, and the London School of Medicine for Women remains the chief centre for the medical education of women in London.

Pharmacy is taught at most of the Universities, but all pharmacists must prepare, at the Universities or in special schools, for examinations held by an outside body—the Pharmaceutical Society. Degrees in Dentistry are conferred by some Universities, and an excellent training is provided, but the profession of Dentistry is still unregulated by the State, and unqualified persons freely practise. This makes Dentistry less popular as a profession among persons of University education; but there is a great field for qualified dentists, and women would do well to enter upon it in larger numbers.

Languages studied at the Universities are Greek, Latin, French, German, Oriental languages, and more recently, Italian, Spanish, and Russian. The teaching in modern languages is carried on partly by native, partly by foreign lecturers; except in Oriental languages, which are practically always taught by Englishmen. There is a tendency observable at present in the Secondary Schools, and in the Universities, to give less attention than hitherto to Greek and Latin.

Faculties of Commerce have been established in the great civic Universities of Birmingham and Manchester, and recently in London; Leeds and Liverpool also give teaching in Commerce. Economics is a subject of study—sometimes the subject of an Honours Schools—in most of the Universities. The London School of Economics has unrivalled facilities for research and advanced study.

In the Fine Arts there is practically no University study. Throughout the country there are Schools of Music, some of which are recognised, as in London and Manchester, as institutions affiliated to the University; but none of them are mainly under University control. The Schools of Art existing in many of the larger cities are also self-governing institutions. A movement has been set on foot for bringing some of these into closer connection with the Universities, and the Slade Art School in London is closely connected with University College; but on the whole very little progress has yet been recorded. The nearest approach to recognition of the existence of the Fine Arts (outside the Slade School), is the establishment of Schools of Art and Architecture in the Universities of Liverpool and Manchester, but these are concerned very largely with Architecture rather than with the Fine Arts.

The study of Law in England is carried on to some extent in the Universities, many of which have Faculties of Law; but the examinations which admit to practice as Barristers are controlled by the Council of Legal Education (established by four ancient foundations, the Inns of Court in London), and those admitting Solicitors are held by the Law Society. Preparation for these examinations is mainly post-graduate, and must, in part at least, be carried on in the Inns of Court or under the Law Society. Colonial and foreign students may, under certain conditions, be admitted. The admission of women is of very recent date. No woman has as yet quite completed all the formalities entitling her to be "called to the Bar"—that is, to be recognised as qualified to plead before the Courts; but a considerable number are now engaged in preparing for the profession, as solicitors or barristers.

The study of Agriculture, Horticulture and kindred subjects is provided for in nearly all the Universities, which maintain their own practical and experimental farms. It is, however, more usual to pursue these studies in various independent colleges, where practical work plays a larger part than scientific training. For women there are, among others, Horticultural Colleges at Swanley and at Studley, and the Edinburgh School of Gardening for Women. These colleges for the most part prepare pupils for the examinations of the Royal Horticultural Society. The University College of Reading makes special provision for education in Horticulture and Agriculture, which is rendered valuable by close co-operation with the Department of Science; and the College awards its own Diploma.

Physical Culture.—Very little attention is at present paid by University authorities to physical training and education, no University giving a professional training in physical culture. For women a number of independent Colleges provide full courses of instruction suited to prepare teachers in the subject; for men teachers there is practically no provision. Any systematic teaching in gymnasium exercise is usually given to men by ex-Army instructors; coaching in games (football, cricket, rowing, etc.), is given by special experts. For a nation which, unofficially, attaches immense importance to physical "fitness" and to athletic games, the neglect of scientific study of the subject, and the absence of official provision for systematic exercise, is astonishing. Universities and Colleges for the most part limit themselves to supporting financially the provision of gymnasium and athletic grounds, where such students as desire if may indulge in open-air games or indoor exercise. In the residential Universities the early part of the afternoon is by common consent left free for recreation; but in the great civic Universities, for the most part non-residential, this is rendered impossible by the necessity for freeing the later afternoon for the return journey of students from a distance. As a result, large numbers of students never take any recreative exercise; and for all of them the possibilities are extremely limited. In these civic Universities, moreover, the athletic grounds are nearly all inevitably situated at a considerable distance from the University buildings. In these circumstances, opportunities for playing games are practically limited to "match teams," the chief game played by women being hockey. The part of the average student is therefore mainly that of an onlooker, and this is likely to continue so, unless the Universities should decide to take more full official direction of the physical development of their students. There are signs of a movement towards this; but the difficulties are great, and very little has been achieved. The Board of Education has set an example by insisting that all students training to be teachers, at the Universities or elsewhere, shall take a minimum of some form of physical exercise.

Social Science.—Several Universities carry on Departments (or Schools) for the study of Social Science, usually in close connection with University Settlements and with such organisations for charity and relief as exist in the district. Women enter these "Schools" in some number; since there are many openings for them as organising secretaries, and some few as investigators into social conditions. Birmingham, Glasgow, and Liverpool are good centres for this study; and the London School of Economics offers an excellent training in methods of research.

Household Economics.—Very little has as yet been done by the Universities for this subject of study. Most of the large cities support Municipal Schools of Domestic Economy; but these are unconnected with the Universities, and give a training which is purely practical. It is much to be desired that encouragement should be given to a more scientific study of questions of nutrition and diet, and methods of institutional management. The only institution of University rank concerning itself with this study is King's College for Women (Household and Social Science Department), London.

The study of Education has already been discussed.

Sessions and Terms.—The whole period of study in any given year is called a Session, and the session usually consists of three terms—Michaelmas, Lent, and Easter (or Summer)—each of about ten or eleven weeks. In Cambridge, however, the terms are about nine weeks each, and in Oxford, eight. Terms in Faculties of Medicine (and Dentistry) are often longer than in other Faculties; and in Scotland, some Faculties still adhere to the old plan of two terms. The session begins in October.

There are vacations at Christmas and at Easter, dividing the terms, and varying in length from a fortnight to four or five weeks. In the Long Vacation (July to September) there is no systematic instruction for the ordinary University student, though from time to time "summer schools" are held for students from outside, more especially in Universities situated in an attractive environment. In Cambridge there is also a Long Vacation term, during which tuition is given, without lectures, to those University students who desire it.

Lectures are usually given and laboratory work done in the morning and afternoon; in Faculties of Commerce there are also evening lectures.

Women on the Staff.—In spite of the fact that, nominally at least, professorial appointments have now been open to women for a good many years, very few women professors have as yet been appointed. There are two or three in Departments of Education; women have quite recently been appointed to professorial chairs in French and Italian; and the National University of Ireland has appointed one or two women. Oxford, opened to women only in 1920, has already a woman as Acting-Professor of French. But the number of women professors is still disappointingly few; and it is difficult to say whether the chief cause is lack of applications from women or prejudice on the part of appointing bodies; both causes undoubtedly operate.

Women lecturers are not so rare, though their numbers are still comparatively small. They are most numerous in Education, but are appointed also in other Faculties, salaries being the same as for men. The main avenue to

University teaching for women lies through the Colleges for women only, where they, of course, form the entire residential staff; the tutorial system of Cambridge and Oxford thus affords employment in higher teaching to a considerable number of women. Further, the residential Halls attached to the mixed Universities provide posts of responsibility and prestige for a considerable number of educated women as Wardens or Principals. The recognition accorded to these officials by the University itself is, however, not always entirely satisfactory.

Upon the whole, the present position of women upon the staffs of the Universities and Colleges is one of comparative subordination. Very few occupy senior posts of importance and prestige. Except in the Women's Colleges, the higher direction of the teaching and the general administration are still almost wholly in the hands of men; and this is the case even where, as in Wales, the number of men and women students is fairly equal.

On account of the comparative scarcity of women in senior positions, it is usual in most non-residential Colleges and Universities to employ some senior woman as a member of the administrative staff, charged with the duty of superintending the general welfare of the women students.[3] Her status and duties vary greatly—from those of a mere chaperon to those of a Senior authority, consulted in all matters concerning women students individually and collectively, and responsible for making representations as to any matter, academic or social, affecting them. It is partially realised that women students, having often received a different education from that given to boys and having the prospect of other careers and other spheres of work, may be specially affected by academic legislation; and in matters of building and equipment their needs are always to some extent special. The most enlightened Universities and Colleges therefore afford considerable powers and status to this woman official (who is known by various titles— Dean, Senior Tutor, Censor, etc). In residential Universities the Heads of the Women's Colleges have the necessary academic information, official status, and knowledge of their students' needs.

Residence.—All Universities and Colleges (except the University of London on its external side) require students to live in the district and to receive instruction or guidance in the institution itself. Certain Universities

---

[3] There are, however, some eight or nine exceptions. The Association of Head Mistresses has asked that some such official shall be appointed wherever there are women students.

and Colleges also require all students to be members of organised bodies, for the most part resident in Colleges or Halls.[4] This is the case in Cambridge and in Oxford. In London, Bedford, Holloway, and Westfield Colleges are largely or mainly residential. The University College of Wales, Aberystwyth, is, for women, entirely residential; and the University College of Reading requires both men and women to live in Halls. All the other Universities (except Aberdeen) have Halls, large or small, for women students, but do not compel residence. Lists of Halls can be obtained from the University prospectuses; and applications for residence (as distinct from entrance to the University) should be made direct to the various Wardens or Principals. The demand for accommodation is everywhere very great; and it is practically impossible to secure admission unless application is made at least a year in advance. It is usually a great additional benefit for foreign students to reside in a Hall; and every effort should be made to secure provisional acceptance beforehand.

Discipline varies from one University to another—from the comparatively strict discipline necessitated in old Universities with a long tradition of obedience and convention; or in smaller Universities which are the centre of interest in small towns such as Reading and Aberystwyth; to the freedom of the great civic University, compelled to accord almost complete social liberty to the large numbers of men and women living in their own homes; and comfortably sheltered from censorious criticism among the many more exciting attractions existing in every great city. In some Universities men and women students may not converse together in the streets; in others they may freely meet, walk, take meals, and study together.

In all Universities and Colleges there is much *Social Intercourse* and gaiety. Dancing is very frequent; dramatic performances, debates (for one sex only, or mixed) are common; and almost every Honours School or Department has its Society for the encouragement of its special subject, and the promotion of social intercourse among its members. Even in Oxford and Cambridge some of these Societies include both men and women.

Residential Colleges and Halls usually provide "Common" (or "Combination") Rooms where staff or students can meet each other; and the mixed Universities set apart rooms, usually separate for men and for women, for

---

[4] In regard to the meaning the terms 'College' and 'Hall,' it may be said that (except in Oxford) the 'Hall' provides residence only; the 'College' provides teaching, and arranges for admission into the University, while it may, or may not, also provide residence.

the hours of the day not devoted to study. These may be simply sitting-rooms with restaurant attached, as in the smaller institutions, or may be, in the more established modern Universities, large, well-furnished Union Buildings or club-houses, as provided in Edinburgh, Liverpool, or Manchester. The management of these Unions, as to both finance and discipline, is usually in the hands of the students themselves. In no University, however, does the *accommodation for women* compare in dignity, commodiousness, or spaciousness with that provided in many American institutions. With the exception of some of the oldest Universities, where the provision for men is ample and beautiful, University and College buildings in Great Britain are upon a wholly different scale from those in the United States. While laboratories are often excellently equipped, libraries and lecture-rooms are not infrequently inadequate, and the provision for recreation, physical well-being, and social intercourse is sometimes seriously wanting. Nothing exists in our modern Universities at all comparable with the magnificent buildings, the extensive grounds, woods and lakes, the immense gymnasiums and swimming baths, provided for women students in the United States. And in the older of our civic Universities, the cramped conditions of existence in the midst of an immense city are responsible for the absence of many social amenities. In the smaller, younger Universities an attempt is being made to secure more space for future development before it is too late; but the standards even there are far below those known in the United States. English girls of aristocratic or wealthy parentage do not as yet go to the University in large numbers; most of the students come from homes of limited means, and their demands, except in the matter of education pure and simple, are modest. At the same time, one never hears of students, as in American Colleges, paying their expenses by giving personal service; it would, in fact, be very difficult for the average student to spare sufficient time from her studies, which are exacting enough to leave her only the minimum amount of leisure essential for recreation.

Finance is a matter for serious concern in our Universities, largely dependent as they are upon small public grants and private benefactions; and in Women's Colleges and Halls this question is still more pressing. It should be remembered that the numbers in our Women's Colleges are small; all the five Women's Colleges together in Oxford do not number 700 students. Moreover, though the generous benefactor exists in this country, his gifts are on a comparatively modest scale, and institutions specially for women do not attract the largest.

Libraries.—The most complete collections of books are those of the privileged libraries, the British Museum Library, the Bodleian (Oxford), the Cambridge University Library, the Advocates' Library (Edinburgh), the Trinity College Library (Dublin), and, more recently, the National Library of Wales. Each of these is privileged to receive a copy of every book published in Great Britain. Other valuable libraries are those of the London School of Economics, and the School of Oriental Studies (London). In Manchester a rich storehouse of early printed books, mediaeval manuscripts, and general literature is provided by the lavishly endowed John Rylands Library, the ancient Chetham Library, the University (Christie) Library, and the Municipal Reference Library.

Expenses.—University education in Great Britain is not free, as in some countries; although in the case of a certain number of students, Government grants or local scholarships cover the expenses more or less completely. It is extremely difficult to give any figures as to the cost of a University training, on account of the great difference in the fees and the general absence of any inclusive charge. It is, moreover, to be noted that, where the University includes several Colleges, there are often both College fees and University fees. The fees for residence in College, again, may or may not include also the fees for tuition and lectures. Life at Cambridge is, for women, rather more expensive than in other Universities; but in Oxford it is less expensive to be a member of the Society of Home Students than to reside in a College, and in Cambridge the small number of older students permitted by the Colleges to be "out-students" can live more cheaply. Again, the extreme brevity of the terms in Cambridge and Oxford entails heavy vacation expenses for the foreign student.

At Oxford and Cambridge the cost of board, lodging and tuition for the session, consisting of three terms of eight to nine weeks each, varies from £135 to £150.

Next in order of expense comes London, where the fees for residence in College, apart from tuition, are £90 to £100. In the larger University cities of England, residence costs about £70; in the smaller places, in Wales and in Scotland, it is lower (£40 to £50).

Where the fees for guidance or tuition in advanced work are charged separately from those for residence, they vary from £5 to £15 in the Faculty of Arts; in the Faculty of Science they usually depend on the nature of the practical work involved. For the examination of these the charge may be from £5 to £10, and for the conferment of the degree from £5 to £20.

Careers for University Women.

Most of the women students in British Universities are intending to earn their living; the exceptions being a few at Oxford and Cambridge. The careers most fully open to them are teaching and medicine, for which full professional training is provided in the Universities. A large army of women graduates is employed in the Secondary Schools, and many women doctors hold positions in hospitals, especially in those for women and children, or carry on private practice. Pharmacy is chosen as an occupation by many women, and in dentistry there is plenty of room—though very few women enter upon it.

Students showing marked talent fairly often obtain grants enabling them to prosecute research for a year or two; a few private commercial firms employ research workers and occasionally engage a woman; but the opportunities of this kind are comparatively rare. A certain number of women in practically every University now hold positions as Demonstrators in laboratories, or as Assistant Lecturers or Lecturers; a very few are Professors. Some are employed as lecturers under organisations for extending advanced teaching outside the Universities.[5]

In the Civil Service (which is the general name for the various departments of work under the Government), University women are employed in some numbers under the Board of Education, the Home Office, the Ministry of Health and the Local Government Board, as Inspectors and Medical Officers. The Ministry of Labour and the Post Office, while employing large numbers of women, offer very few posts suitable for University graduates. During the war many women held in Government offices positions of importance and responsibility; but most of them have now been dispensed

[5] Such are the Workers' Educational Association, and the various University Extension Schemes.

with under the plea of economy, or of providing employment for discharged soldiers. A very few of these women, however, still retain their posts, and there is a fairly powerful movement for opening the higher positions in the Civil Service to women. Hitherto all women employed have been engaged by individual selection; it is now proposed that after three years from 1921, they shall be eligible to compete for posts in the same examinations as men, though power is to be retained to appoint to any given post either a man or a woman, as may seem best, from among the successful candidates. It remains to be seen to what extent this provision may be used to nullify the chances of women. There is powerful opposition in many Government departments; but the Treasury is said to be favourable to the gradual introduction of women in higher administrative positions. At present, such openings for them are few. It is not at present even proposed to open to them positions in diplomacy or in the consulate.

A considerable number of educated women find administrative positions as Heads of University Colleges, Halls of Residence, and Training Colleges for Teachers. Some of the older Training Colleges are still presided over by men as Principals; but it is the policy of the Board of Education to replace these upon retirement by women. All Heads and Assistants in Elementary and Secondary Schools for girls only are women; but in schools open to both boys and girls, it is customary to appoint a man as Head, with or without a senior woman in special charge of the girls. In Scotland it is still common for a girls' school to have a Headmaster.

Secretarial work is a career coveted by many University graduates unwilling to enter upon the occupation of teaching. The Universities do not, however, provide a professional training for this; nor are the openings suited for University women very numerous. Some occasionally find congenial posts as foreign correspondents in banks and commercial firms; many become organising secretaries for philanthropic or kindred organisations; a favoured few become private secretaries to literary, scientific, or political personages. The demand, however, for secretaries of University education is not at this moment equal to the supply.

The Church offers at present very little scope for women: except in one or two of the free sects, the ministry is not open to them. The Law has only within the last year or two been opened to them.

Librarianship offers a very limited number of opportunities. Some College and University libraries employ a few women in comparatively subordinate positions; the ordinary City Library does not offer any opening to women of University education. An attempt has recently been made to provide a professional training for Librarians, following the example set long ago by the United States; but for women the prospects seem at present precarious.

Home Economics and Domestic Science being (with the exception noted above) still outside the purview of the Universities, practically no University women are qualified to undertake posts either as teachers or as practical workers in this sphere. There is, however, a very large demand for highly qualified Institutional Managers, Matrons, Superintendents, etc., and good salaries can be earned in such positions. It is to be hoped that with the return of better financial prospects in the Universities, advanced training in work of this kind, eminently suitable for educated women, may be undertaken.

It will be seen that, though many careers are open to University women, the prizes are few; and in very many of these careers the openings are so rare, or the initial income offered so low, that only those who are adventurous or independent financially, can afford to run the risk involved in choosing them. By far the most usual occupation for them, apart from medicine, is the profession of teaching; although it is now by no means, as at one time, the only avenue open. During the war, women teachers entered boys' schools in considerable numbers, but, except for quite young boys, few of these are now retained. Upon the whole, the outlook is discouraging to those who looked for a permanent increase in the number of openings for women as a result of women's varied services in the war. Only a few positions of importance have been retained, and throughout the whole field of labour women have lost the greater part of the advance made. All that seems to be definitely gained at present is the breaking down of the bar of absolute exclusion.

Women Students from Other Countries.

Women students wishing to enter any University in Great Britain should have complete command of the English language, since this is pre-supposed in all University studies. In none of the Universities is any course arranged specially for foreign students (though occasionally summer schools suitable for foreigners are held); but, provided they can pass the Entrance Examinations, foreigners are accepted as students in the ordinary courses. It is not, however, as a rule very practicable for a foreigner to pass one of these Entrance Examinations—planned as they are for British boys and girls leaving school. By far the best plan is to study first at a home University and resort to this country only for post-graduate work. The student should forward to the proper authority (usually the Registrar) an application for admission giving full information as to her previous University studies, with examinations passed, etc.; and each application is usually considered entirely upon its merits. As a rule, any candidate who can give proof of having attained a standard equivalent to that of the first degree examination may hope for admission without further test. The studies of all such post-graduate students are directed individually by the Professor of the subject concerned; and it is advisable to communicate with him before actually applying for admission to the College or University. The most suitable degree for such students to work for is the Ph.D., open in any Faculty. Nearly all Universities publish special prospectuses giving details as to the facilities provided for research and advanced work.

Scholarships and Fellowships.—There is only one Fellowship definitely set aside to be awarded to foreign students—the John W. Garrett International Fellowship in Bacteriology, offered by the University of Liverpool to students from the United States or other foreign countries. In several Universities, however, scholarships and fellowships exist which are not limited to students in Great Britain; and particulars of these can be obtained from their Scholarship Prospectuses. Candidates from other countries must, however, produce ample proof of their qualifications, and are probably at some disadvantage unless they have studied under professors of world-wide reputation. In many of the Universities there are endowments for research open to persons, whether British born or not, who have already begun work at the University in question.

Appendix.

The British Federation of University Women.

President:

Professor Caroline Spurgeon, Doc. Univ. Paris,
Hon. Litt.D. (Michigan).

The British Federation of University Women was formed in 1910, for the purpose of furthering the interests of University women.

Aims of the Federation.

1. To create an organisation which shall represent University women in *all* professions, and enable them to take concerted action on matters affecting their interests in public and private life.

2. To promote co-operation between the University women of Great Britain, and to stimulate friendship between University women throughout the world.

3. To encourage independent research work by University women.

4. To stimulate the interest of University women in municipal and public life.

5. To keep a Register of University women and to notify them of suitable appointments.

Constitution.

The British Federation is composed of Local Associations of University women, the country being divided for this purpose into areas around different large centres. Local Associations have been formed in eleven areas, the centre in each case being a University town. Twenty members is the minimum required to form a Local Association. These Associations are free to adopt any objects which are in accord with the "Aims of the Federation."

Membership.

Membership is restricted to women who hold a University degree or its equivalent. Registered medical women or registered dentists are qualified for membership.

In addition to regular members the Federation admits as associates, in certain cases, women who have studied for not less than two years regularly at a University. Students in their last year may be admitted as temporary associates, at the discretion of the Local Association, on the understanding that they become members after taking their degree.

Women who have not studied at a University, but who have advanced the higher education and the interests of women, may be admitted by the Local Associations as honorary members.

Neither associates nor honorary members have voting power.

Annual Meeting.

An Annual Meeting of the General Committee is held during the summer term for the election of the officers of the Federation and other business. This General Committee is composed of the members of the Executive Committee and delegates from each Local Association.

Special meetings may also be called at the request of the delegates of any three branches.

Executive Committee.

The Executive Committee consists of the President, Hon. Secretaries,

Hon. Treasurer, the Chairman of the Committee on International Relations, the Secretaries of the British Federation and of the Committee on International Relations, eight members elected by the General Committee at the Annual Meeting, and representatives of each Local Association. The Executive may co-opt four additional members.

The President may not hold office for more than five years, and the eight elected members of the Executive retire annually. No member of the Executive Committee, other than the officers, may hold office for more than four consecutive years.

Finance.

Members are admitted to Local Associations on payment of a small entrance fee (6d.) and either an annual subscription, varying slightly within the different Associations, or a uniform life membership subscription of £3 10s. Annual subscriptions are paid to the local secretaries or treasurers. Life subscriptions are paid to the central Treasurer. Each Local Association contributes out of its annual subscriptions a minimum capitation fee of 4s. per member to the general funds of the Federation. The financial year runs from June 1st to May 31st.

The Central Office of the Federation is at 73, Avenue Chambers, Vernon Place, Southampton Row, London, W.C.1.